T0132226

Proverbial Kids

Lesson PLANS for Parents

Featuring 7 ABCs of Wisdom from Proverbs

By Karen Anderson Holcomb

Proverbial Kids©
Wisdom for Young Families

THE HOLY BIBLE, NEW INTERNATIONAL VERSION®, NIV® Copyright © 1973, 1978, 1984, 2011 by Biblica, Inc.® Used by permission. All rights reserved worldwide.

WestBow Press books may be ordered through booksellers or by contacting:

WestBow Press
A Division of Thomas Nelson & Zondervan
1663 Liberty Drive
Bloomington, IN 47403
www.westbowpress.com
1 (866) 928-1240

Because of the dynamic nature of the Internet, any web addresses or links contained in this book may have changed since publication and may no longer be valid. The views expressed in this work are solely those of the author and do not necessarily reflect the views of the publisher, and the publisher hereby disclaims any responsibility for them.

Any people depicted in stock imagery provided by Getty Images are models, and such images are being used for illustrative purposes only.
Certain stock imagery © Getty Images.

ISBN: 978-1-9736-4363-0 (sc)
ISBN: 978-1-9736-4364-7 (e)

Library of Congress Control Number: 2018912794

Print information available on the last page.

WestBow Press rev. date: 12/14/2018

"Listen, my son, to your father's instruction, and don't reject your mother's teaching, for they will be a garland of grace on your head and a gold chain around your neck."

Proverbs 1:8-9 (CSB)

Introduction

Americans have long been enamored with fictional superhero characters who battle to defend the earth against evil threats. From the first *Superman* movie in 1938 to today's marvels and avengers, we have seen more than 80 years of ever-increasing power and intelligence played out on the big screen, all for our protection. Yet within those same decades, American family life has imploded. Home is no longer a safe base. Debt, divorce, discord, chaotic scheduling, addiction—all point to the need for protective moral and spiritual principles which carry us from childhood into adulthood, boundaries which protect our children and infuse peace into our homes. I believe the supernatural God of our nonfictional universe has some 3,000-year-old principles to combat today's "new normal" problems!

In Old Testament Bible times, two men whose names also began with an "S" were the real thing—superheroes, given supernatural abilities by God Himself. *Samson* was given supernatural strength (Judges 13-16). *Solomon* was given supernatural wisdom (1 Kings 3). Samson's life and influence was short-lived, but Solomon's influence spans millennia.

The book of Proverbs is a 31-chapter collection of wise sayings, practical advice for skillful & godly living, written almost entirely by King Solomon. So broad is the scope of content in Proverbs, one would be hard-pressed to surface a basic life issue which this book does not address. No matter the topic, there is "an app for that." While the verses in Chapters 1-9 and 31 are organized into topics, most of the remaining chapters contain wide assortments of proverbs—prompting the reader to search for the nugget of the day.

This Proverbial Kids lesson-plan book is a tool for discovering and applying God's wisdom in Proverbs to your family life. As a parent, curriculum writer, and former children's minister, I've identified seven ABCs of wisdom in Proverbs, recurring themes which speak God's wisdom into the conflicts we face early on in parenting. On the following pages, you will find a synopsis of the seven themes and a simple two-page lesson plan for each ABC. A handful of Proverbs verses are listed for your study, along with parallel principles from the 10 Commandments and verses from the book of James.

You decide how you will use this resource—family devotions, small groups, homeschooling, children's church or camp! Pick and choose from four opening activities, four different Bible stories, for as many as 28 one-hour sessions and hundreds of teaching moments. Object lessons and discussion questions are included. For each theme, I have written and illustrated a colorful "character" book for parents to read with their children, also available through Westbow Press. All Proverbial Kids materials are available digitally, making it easy to follow God's directive in Deuteronomy 6:7 for "on the road" parenting! I hope they are helpful to you!

Karen Holcomb

*"If any of you lacks wisdom, he should ask God, who gives generously
to all without finding fault, and it will be given to him."*

James 1:5

7 ABCs of Wisdom from Proverbs

 ## Accept Instruction

Proverbs 1 introduces the vast collection of King Solomon's wise sayings with a five-verse purpose statement. They are for *growth*, *insight*, *character-building*, *shrewdness vs. naivete*, and *mature & deep thinking*. The Proverbs were written for parenting! Urging his own son to accept his mother's and father's instructions in verse 8, Solomon indicates victorious results in verse 9, "they will be a garland of grace on your head and a gold chain around your neck." Garland and gold are for champions, and we know that champions are not born overnight! Look inside the word *instruction* and you will discover the Latin word *struct*, meaning "to build". As you fairly and consistently teach your sons and daughters and they follow your guidance, a structure is being built inside them for wise living. Train your unique children to accept instruction and watch them rise to become champions!

 ## Be Humble and Kind

Humility has been defined as having a realistic opinion of oneself. That's a tall order in today's selfie-, superhero-driven world. Acknowledging our own human limitations leads us to be gracious with others, to be less critical and more kind. The prefixes *hum* and *kin* are rooted in people! As you encourage your children in their strengths and weaknesses, in their successes and failures, help them see the good in other people as well. Proverbs 6, 8, and 19 tell us that God detests arrogance, that pride brings disgrace, and that kindness toward people is in fact kindness toward God. Teach humility and kindness early in your child's life. Zoom out as you video your kids' ballgames and concerts. Give freely. Temper an air of arrogance with realism and objectivity. Resist the urge to worship your children! Remind your own self to be humble and to be kind, and rest in the awesome promise that God has a plan for each human life—all for His glory.

 ## Control Your Curiosity & Your Tongue

At the heart of any lesson on self-control is the principle of living within boundaries. Jesus referred to sin as a *trespass* in Matthew 6. This word is most often used today to mark boundary lines. *No Trespassing* signs clearly distinguish what is mine and what is not mine! Yet, curiosity often lures us to trespass visible and invisible lines. Proverbs 5 encourages young men to stay on a path of safe and righteous living, to drink water from their own wells. Proverbs 8 beautifully describes God's boundary-setting act of Creation. And Proverbs 25:2-3 indicates that God has concealed certain matters which He alone authorizes revealing through "kings." Entire chapters of Proverbs focus on controlling the tongue—a habitual offender which trespasses against others and sometimes even against oneself! Teach your children that God created boundaries for peace, safety, and liberty. Encourage them to use their curiosity and words for good and not for evil!

 ## Don't Be Lazy or Rude

King Solomon enjoyed nature and animals. 1 Kings 4:32-33 tells us, "He described trees, from the cedar in Lebanon to the hyssop growing out of the wall. He also taught about animals, birds, reptiles, and fish." It's no wonder he took note of the tiny ant's work ethic in Proverbs 6. Laziness was a pet peeve of the hard-working monarch, and God gave him much insight about lazy people—their lack of initiative, wastefulness, and propensity to sleep too much. Consequently, they have terrible reputations and their futures are "blocked with thorns" (15:19). Parents are responsible for teaching children how to work hard and be respectful of others. Proverbs 29:21 says, "A servant pampered from youth will turn out to be insolent." With arrogant rudeness, he will come to expect special treatment and undeserved privileges. In teaching our kids to work hard, we need to keep home, family, church, and community responsibilities high on our list, rather than just those activities which are child-centered (sports, dance, etc.). Invite God to help you establish a well-balanced schedule and priority set as a family. This will keep laziness and rudeness at bay.

 ## Enjoy God's Wisdom

Our Creator God is both sovereign and relational. His wisdom is vast, extending across all subject matters. He poured insightful knowledge into King Solomon about the plant and animalworld, construction, leadership and government, and wisdom regarding human behavior and relationships. If anyone could come to trust his own understanding, it would have been Solomon. Yet, in Proverbs 3:5-6 Solomon urged his son to acknowledge and trust God for direction in life. As you teach your children to enjoy God's wisdom, begin with Creation and trace His marvelous thread of redemption through Jesus Christ. Use Proverbs to teach them to love others, to do good and avoid evil. Emphasize God's love and the protection that comes through obeying Him.

 ## Forfeit Fortune and Fame

The American Dream has grown big and cumbersome in recent decades, adversely affecting family life. This "F" principle challenges us to forfeit material wealth and self-centered popularity for a more rewarding life that values Family, Faith, and Friendship. Proverbs pits the pursuit of fortune and fame against family life consistently, and you will appreciate the wisdom highlighted in this lesson plan. Making a name for oneself, the pursuit of wealth, deferring your child's hope, working too hard, contentious and strife-filled homes, wonder-lust, pride and selfishness—all 21st Century topics are addressed in this 3,000-year-old collection. Thankfully, there is a path to joy through God's wisdom! As you teach your children what is really important in life, invite God to fine-tune your priorities. Help your sons and daughters forfeit fortune and fame for faith, family, and friendship. Then enjoy deserved attention and reward with joyful gratitude!

 ## Gain Honestly

Gaining is a necessary part of life. Our bodies live off the intake of food and the protection of clothing and shelter. We gain things, favor, stature, friendships, responsibilities, knowledge, and the money necessary for trade in civilization. God created us to be industrious, hard-working, energy-burning beings. And He created the moral law which favors honest gain. Chapters 6, 11, and 12 of Proverbs reveal valuable principles about *gain:* deceitful gain breeds disaster, kindness gains honor, generosity leads to gain, fantasy-chasing does not produce gain, and hard work is gainfully rewarding. Add to that 11:1, "The LORD detests dishonest scales," and 21:6, "a fortune made by a lying tongue is a fleeting vapor and a deadly snare." In contrast to our "F" principle, this plan teaches honest, necessary gain. This principle will be a great lesson for your children who love to trade toys, games, and favors. It emphasizes honesty in all they say and do.

As you review these seven ABC principles, you will discover they are interrelated, with two common denominators: love for God and love for others (Mark 12:30-31). Where King Solomon failed later in life to keep God first, God's own Son persevered to the cross, sinless. Jesus Christ is the power and wisdom of God (1 Cor. 1:30-31), the perfect balancing ransom for a guilt-weighted world. God bless you and your family as you dive into His wisdom!

Plans
and
Proverbs

7 Plans for as many as 28 one-hour sessions
and hundreds of teaching moments!

TEACHING PLAN – A

Welcome! Read the following plan carefully, along with the topical paragraph on page (v). Prayerfully select one Opening Activity and one Bible Lesson to lead. Record Proverbs passages on a separate sheet. Begin with the Activity, share the Key Verse and the Bible story. Supplement with the Object Lesson and Q & A. Obtain the character storybook suggested below to read aloud with your children.

Accept Instruction

Key Verse: *Listen, my son, to your father's instruction, and don't reject your mother's teaching, for they will be a garland of grace on your head and a gold chain around your neck.* Proverbs 1:8-9 (CSB)

Opening Activity—Follow Instructions! Choose one activity.

Gold Medal Course— Set up and host an obstacle course competition with gold, silver, and bronze awards.

Blind-folded Tour— Pair up! Blindfold one partner; direct the other to guide him/her on a 10-minute tour.

Toy-making/building— Put together an interlocking toy set or other DIY item, referring to instructions.

Cooking— Select several new recipes and prepare each dish, with a different family member as the head chef.

Bible Lesson Choose one story.

Read the passage and highlights noted on the adjacent page; prepare to tell the story in your own words. Discuss, using the Q & A guide below. Share the Key Verse (above) and other related Proverbs. Say, **God wants you to respect and obey your parents. Following their instructions will bring you great reward!**

- ♦ *God's Parenting*— Genesis 1 and 2
- ♦ *Noah's Ark*— Genesis 6:9-22, 7 & 8
- ♦ *Abraham's Journey*— Genesis 12:1-9
- ♦ *David's Army*— 1 Chronicles 12

Object Lesson

Show the following items and ask, **How may each of these be used in giving and/or following instructions?**

Measuring Tape

Notepad & Pencil

Sheet Music

Road Map

Toolbox with Tools

Work Gloves

Role Play a situation in which one of these props is necessary for success.

Q & A

⇒ Who is the leader in this story?
⇒ Name some of the *instructions* in this Bible passage & their good purpose.
⇒ What could be some consequences of not following these instructions?

Note: God is glorified in our obedience!

Character Book

Little Jimmy and the Spoiled Rotten Banana is the story of a young boy who cries and throws tantrums to get what he wants. When an unwise purchase results in a broken arm, Jimmy's parents turn to the book of Proverbs for wisdom. They discover a firm "No" is foundational in parenting.

More stories and resources available at karenholcombbooks.com and proverbialkids.com.

♦ God's Parenting— Genesis 1 and 2

God made man on the sixth day of Creation. As his Heavenly Father, God provided Adam with food and a home. Seeing Adam's social needs, He **gave him a complementary companion**. He **gave work and home instructions** to Adam and Eve in Genesis 1:27-28 and **boundaries and opportunities** to Adam in 2:17, 19. God **revealed His love** for them by visiting them in the evenings. When Adam and Eve disobeyed Him, He **gave them a chance to confess**, sacrificially **forgave** them, **enforced consequences**, and **remained in relationship** with them. As you share the story of Creation and the first family with your children, help them understand the pattern God set in leadership, which He expects wise parents and children to follow. Share Proverbs 1:8-9 with your kids; encourage them to accept instruction like champions!

♦ Noah's Ark— Genesis 6:9-22, 7, 8

When God decided to destroy the corrupt earth with a flood, He gave Noah some very specific instructions! Introduce this story with its basic facts, then read Genesis 6:9-22 aloud to your family. Enlist a family member to create a list on a dry erase board of all the instructions God gave Noah—starting with #1: Build an Ark. Point out the specific numbers in many of the instructions and the risk of not following these instructions carefully. Share the "rest of the story" from chapter 7 and remark how even the sky and earth obeyed God's command to flood the planet. Rejoice that Noah's family was kept alive because they accepted instruction from God!

♦ Abraham's Journey— Genesis 12:1-9

Sometimes, we have to accept instruction with "blind faith"! Abram was a good man, a descendant of Noah's son Shem. He was a family man, growing up in the city of Ur, then moving with his father's entire family to Haran. Genesis 12 records God's call to Abram to leave his relatives and travel to an unknown destination. Read Genesis 12:1-9 aloud or tell the encounter in your own words. Exclaim how this instruction must have surprised Abram! Lead your family members to consider how they would respond to such an order—the workload, the uncertainty, the people they would miss. Share Gen. 15:1-7. God kept His promises to Abram—a new homeland, a son with Sarah, the blessed nation of Israel as his descendants and other nations, too. God changed his name to Abraham, meaning *father of many nations.*

♦ David's Army— 1 Chronicles 12

An exciting passage, 1 Chronicles 12:1-22 describes the special military forces who were David's defense against King Saul, with verses 23-37 describing those who defected to David upon Saul's death. Verse 38 binds them as a solid force en route to Hebron to make David king. Explain the scenario to your kids, emphasizing verses 2, 8, and 16-18. Show them the large numbers of defectors in 24-37. How did David lead all these men? God gave him 30 mighty commanders and thousands of warriors who could "keep rank." Read aloud verse 38. Explain how important it is for soldiers to accept instruction from their superiors. Victory is achieved as we do so, honoring our leaders wholeheartedly!

Find these verses in your Bible and write them on a separate sheet.

Proverbs

3:11-12
6:23
10:17
13:13
15:32
19:18
22:6

See also 10 Commandments #1 & #5 and James 1:5 and 1:21-22.

Instruct your children this week in these areas:

Physical Safety
Diet & Nutrition
Bedtime, Rest, & Hygeine
Media Time & Content
Speech

Use God's parenting model (above) as you give instruction and encouragement!

Welcome! Read the following plan carefully, along with the topical paragraph on page (v). Prayerfully select one Opening Activity and one Bible Lesson to lead. Record Proverbs passages on a separate sheet. Begin with the Activity, share the Key Verses and the Bible story. Supplement with the Role Play and Q & A. Obtain the character storybook suggested below to read aloud with your children.

Be Humble & Kind

Key Verse: *Let another praise you, and not your own mouth; someone else, and not your own lips.* Proverbs 27:2
Whoever is kind to the poor lends to the LORD. Proverbs 19:17

Opening Activity— Only Human! Choose one activity.

Reality Check— Measure each person's Long Jump, then the World Record (27'9"), to illustrate human limits.

Show & Tell— Give each family/group member a chance to share a favorite toy, tool, clothing, or talent.

Big Name?— Provide pens and S, M, L, & XL paper (1/person) to make name tags. Discuss equal worth in God's sight.

Secret Service— Draw names and do a secret act of kindness for that person. (i.e., carry, clean, give gift, repair)

Bible Lesson Choose one story.

Read the passage and highlights noted on the adjacent page; prepare to tell the story in your own words. Invite children to share how they may have acted in a similar situation. Define *humble* as having a realistic opinion of yourself. Use the Key Verses, other Proverbs verses and the Q &A below to supplement your teaching.

- ◆ *Mary's Praise—* Luke 1:26-49; 2:17-19
- ◆ *Isaac's Wells—* Genesis 26:12-30
- ◆ *Neb's Brag—* Daniel 4
- ◆ *A Mom's Request—* Matthew 20:20-28

Role Play

Option 1:

Together, write or improvise a paraphrased script of the Bible story you studied, and invite family/group members to act out this brief drama. Use towels, cloths, or robes as costume pieces, and props as needed.

Option 2:

Help children think of everyday situations in which they are tempted to be proud, selfish, or unkind. Act out a modern "drama" that is similar to your Bible story conflict.

Q & A

⇒ Who is this story about?
⇒ Was this person *humble* or *proud*, *kind* or *selfish*? Explain.
⇒ Why is it important to be humble and kind?

Note: No human being is perfect; only God is worthy of glory!

Character Book

Look-at-Me Lucy and the Rearview Mirror is a colorfully-illustrated story of a five-year-old girl who enjoys the attention of family and friends. When it is time to start dance lessons, however, she discovers friendship is better than stardom. Her mother uses the small but wide rearview mirror in their car and several verses from Proverbs to teach a valuable lesson about humility and true beauty that glorifies God.

More stories and resources available at
karenholcombbooks.com **and** proverbialkids.com.

Be Humble & Kind Bible Stories

◆ Mary's Praise— Luke 1:26-38; 1:46-49; 2:17-19

It was the hope of all Jewish young women that they would be the mother of God's Messiah. He chose humble, quiet Mary. Luke 2:1-14 tells of the birth of Jesus. In the surrounding verses we see glimpses of His mother Mary's character. Share the story in Luke 1:26-38 with your children, pointing out her feelings and her humility, gratefully referring to herself as God's slave. In 46-55, Mary's praise reveals her deep, mature faith in God. After Jesus was born and the shepherds came and told Mary and Joseph about the angelic announcement, Mary "treasured up" this news in her heart and quietly meditated on it (2:19). She was not a show-off! Mary magnified God and had a realistic opinion of herself.

◆ Isaac's Wells— Genesis 26:12-30

Successful people tend to have enemies! Abraham's son Isaac settled in the land of Gerar, which was occupied by the Philistines. He sowed seed there and harvested one hundred times what he had planted. Genesis 26:12-14 tells of his vast flocks and herds. He had many hard-working servants, some of whom were very good at digging wells—a special skill in a land that often suffered drought. Jealous, the Philistines would fill Isaac's wells with dirt or claim them as their own. Humbly, Isaac yielded to his enemy neighbor on numerous occasions, moving to new territory. Verses 22-33 tell how God's blessing and Isaac's continued humility and kindness prompted the Philistine king to request a treaty.

◆ Neb's Brag— Daniel 4

History records the greatness of Babylonian King Nebuchadnezzar. His conquests, fortifications and buildings, and extensive gardening and canal systems were renown. Though he had been warned through a dream (interpreted by Daniel) to recognize the Most High God as sovereign or face punishment, Nebuchadnezzar did not. Daniel himself urged the king to repent from sin and turn to righteousness, showing mercy to the poor. Daniel 4:29-37 records the famous king's boast, immediate judgment, and later restoration. True to the dream, he suffered a horrible period of madness, grazing in a field like an animal with bird claws, until his understanding returned and he gave God the glory due His name.

◆ A Mom's Request— Matthew 20:20-28

On His way to Jerusalem where He would be crucified, Jesus was approached by the mother of James and John. She knelt and asked that her sons be given the seats on either side of Him in His kingdom. Jesus responded evenly, but the disciples were indignant over her request! Perhaps they, too, wanted these royal positions! Jesus told them to follow His example, to humble themselves and serve each other, to let others go ahead of them. His words in Matthew 20:23 echo Daniel's in Dan. 2:21, that it is God who puts people in high positions for His purposes. As a family, determine to be humble and kind toward others, trusting God with your ambitions.

Find these verses in your Bible and write them on a separate sheet.

Proverbs

3:3-4
6:16-18
11:2
12:25
14:21
15:1, 33
22:4, 9
31:30-31

See also 10 Commandment #2 & #8 and James 1:9-10, 4:6 & 10.

HOMEWork for Parents

Teach your children to be humble and kind this week as you:

-point out others' talents
-include others in photos
-share
-give to the poor & needy
-spread cheer & encouragement
-curb bragging

Welcome! Read the following plan carefully, along with the topical paragraph on page (v). Prayerfully select one Opening Activity and one Bible Lesson to lead. Record Proverbs passages on a separate sheet. Begin with the Activity, share the Key Verses and the Bible story. Supplement with the Object Lesson and Q & A. Obtain the character storybook suggested below to read aloud with your children.

Control Your Curiosity & Your Tongue

Key Verses: *Drink water from your own cistern, running water from your own well. Proverbs 5:15*
He who holds his tongue is wise. Proverbs 10:19b

Opening Activity— Control Yourself! Choose one activity.

Black Box— Hide something in a box. Give participants 5 minutes to guess item. Introduce topic of curiosity.

Simon Says & Freeze Tag— Play several rounds of either game to illustrate to children their own body control.

Dictionary Search— Pair up! Give each team a hard copy dictionary. Compete to find 6-8 words from your Bible lesson.

Tongue Twisters— Teach your favorite tongue twister! Or, teach family/group members to say their names in Pig Latin.

Bible Lesson Choose one story.

Read the passage and highlights noted on the adjacent page; prepare to tell the story in your own words. (The Job verses focus on his friends' discouraging words.) Use Proverbs verses and the Q & A below to supplement your teaching.

- ♦ **Eve's Choice—** Genesis 3:1-6
- ♦ **Esther's Secret—** Esther 2:15-3:6; 7:1-8:2
- ♦ **Job's Friends—** Job 1; 4:7-8; 8:4; 20:4-5; 33:1-12
- ♦ **Peter's Question—** John 21:21-22

Object Lesson

Display the following item(s) or a picture of the item. Say: **In the New Testament, James says that our tongues are like a:**

Horse's Bit/Ship's Rudder

Flame/Small Fire

Poison/Water Spout

Fig Tree/Grapevine

Lead children to identify each. Explain these concepts from James 3: *1) we need to control our words, 2) our words affect the direction of our lives, 3) words spread from person to person, and 4) loving God leads us to love others in our speech.*

Q & A

⇒ Who is this story about?
⇒ Which did they not control—their tongue or their curiosity? (or both)
⇒ Whom did they hurt or offend by being out of control?

Note: Self-control is a Fruit of the Spirit. As we grow, it should increase!

Character Books

Captain Curious and the Invisible Boundary Line is a story about a little boy named Jasper whose curiosity knows no bounds. When he is drawn into his neighbor's yard, past the No Trespassing sign, Captain Curious gets more than he bargained for. Verses from Proverbs speak wisdom into the conflict, providing delightful teaching moments for parents.

Stories like *Verbose Verbena's Backfire Advice* and more resources available at karenholcombbooks.com and proverbialkids.com.

Control Your Curiosity & Your Tongue **Bible Stories**

◆ Eve's Choice— Genesis 3:1-6

Curiosity can be a great motivation for discovery, but *selfish* curiosity is destructive! Genesis 3 tells us the cunning serpent Satan tempted Eve to eat fruit from the one tree God had forbidden. Eve was curious to taste something new, to own a beautiful forbidden thing, to improve herself to the level of God. Throwing caution to the wind, Eve reached out, plucked a piece of fruit from the branch, and took a bite … then shared it with Adam. How foolish she must have felt later when she realized she had been deceived! No magical taste or beauty, no equality with God, just guilt and loss of relationship. As you share this story with your children, point out that Jesus exercised wisdom and self-control when tempted by the devil in Matthew 4, quoting truths from Scripture to combat the enemy's lie.

◆ Esther's Secret— Esther 2:15-3:6; 7:1-8:2

Sometimes, we must keep private information to ourselves until it is God's time to reveal it. Queen Esther kept a secret from her husband King Xerxes for a short period of time. Xerxes was the king of Persia. By God's divine will, Esther won a beauty contest to be his wife! She did not tell him she was Jewish, because her uncle Mordecai had warned her not to tell. The Jews had enemies in the Persian kingdom who sought to kill them! One day, Mordecai saved the king's life, but the evil officer Haman was rewarded. When Mordecai would not bow to him, Haman became angry and set out to kill all of the Jewish people, whom he hated. At the right time, Esther revealed her identity to King Xerxes and begged his intervention. As you share this story, help your children discern good and bad times to tell private information.

◆ Job's Friends— Job 1; 4:7-8; 8:4; 20:4-5; 33:1-12 (Option: The Israelites' Complaint—Numbers 13 and 14)

Controlling your tongue means more than not saying bad words! We are to control what we say, how we say it, and to whom we say it. Job's friends Eliphaz, Bildad, Zophar, & later Elihu were good examples of bad tongue-control. They saw their friend suffering and assumed they had all the facts about his situation. Little did they know the devil was behind Job's demise. Verses 2:11-13 set the stage for his friends' visit. After seven days, they lit into him with a barrage of words—judgmental, impatient, discouraging speeches. (Share examples of the men's speeches with your kids, showing them the long texts.) Although they said some positive things about God, they were not motivated by love or privy to the spiritual battle taking place. God confronted them about their speech and demanded an apology (42:7-10).

◆ Peter's Question— John 21:21-22 (Option: A Ship's Rudder—James 3:4-5)

"It's none of your bees-wax!" Telling someone to mind his own business can be uncomfortable, but Jesus did just that in John 21. It was His third appearance to the disciples after His resurrection, early in the morning. Jesus cooked breakfast for them and directed them where to catch fish. After breakfast, He restored and re-commissioned the disciple Peter (who had denied Him three times at the crucifixion), prophesying that in his old age Peter would be led to a place he did not want to go. Looking around and seeing John, Peter asked "What about him?" Jesus responded, "What is that to you?" When faced with difficulty, we tend to become insecure and compare ourselves with others! We may be tempted to badmouth or gossip. Faith in God without peer comparison helps us control our curiosity & our tongue!

Find these verses in your Bible and write them in the space provided or on a separate sheet.

Proverbs

5:5,7-8	16:13 (tongue)
6:2 (tongue)	20:19 (tongue)
8:29-30	22:28
10:6-19 (tongue)	25:17
11:12-13 (tongue)	26:17
12:18 (tongue)	27:20

See also 10 Commandment #3, #7 & #9 and James 1:14, 3:1-12.

HOMEWork for Parents

Practice self-control this week by setting limits for your family on:

-social media
-gossip/others' business
-unhealthy physical pleasure
- speech (topic, tone, amount)
-ownership & personal space

Welcome! Read the following plan carefully, along with the topical paragraph on pages (v-vi). Prayerfully select one Opening Activity and one Bible Lesson to lead. Record Proverbs passages on a separate sheet. Begin with the Activity, share the Key Verses and the Bible story. Supplement with the Picture Play or Object Lesson and Q & A. Obtain the character storybook suggested below to read aloud with your children.

Don't be Lazy or Rude

Key Verses: *Lazy hands make for poverty, but diligent hands bring wealth.* Proverbs 10:4
A servant pampered from youth will turn out to be insolent. Proverbs 29:21

Opening Activity— Get it Together! Choose one activity.

Ant Inspection— Start your own ant farm or find a hill of ants outside. Observe them & note their dutiful behavior.

Excuses, Excuses— Pair up! In 3 minutes, list excuses made for not working. Tally unrepeated excuses for winning team.

Mind Your Manners— Play a competitive board game, awarding stickers for polite words and gestures.

No Grumpy Grace— Hunger & fatigue are agitators! Create a kitchen "blessing" mural. Be consistent w/meal & bed times!

Bible Lesson Choose one story.

Read the passage & highlights noted on the adjacent page; prepare to tell it in your own words. (Note: The first two stories are historical accounts about rude men. The second two are *parables* about being diligent.) Use the Key Verses, Proverbs, and the Q & A below to supplement your teaching.

- ◆ **Cain's Attitude—** Genesis 4:1-15
- ◆ **Nabal's Insults—** 1 Samuel 25:2-42
- ◆ **3 Men's Talents—** Matthew 25:14-30
- ◆ **10 Girls' Lamps—** Matthew 25:1-13

Picture Play

Pair up, and make sure each couple has a camera. Setting a timer, give each pair 15 minutes to go take posed pictures of one partner caught in the act of being 1) Lazy, 2) Rude, 3) Diligent, 4) Polite.

Urge them to be creative, using props and facial/body language. When the timer sounds, come back together to share photos & discuss.

Object Lesson

Display a **heavy chain** and discuss how one weak (lazy) link can render it useless for a variety of jobs.

Q & A

⇒ Who is this story about? (tell both good/diligent & rude/lazy characters)
⇒ Describe/List the personalities of the different people in this story.
⇒ What were the consequences of their actions?

Character Books

Lazy Leo's Totally Untapped Talent is the story of a young boy who discovers his hidden talent the day his video game controller flies away, his recliner breaks, and his mom tells him to fix his own problem. Verses from Proverbs direct his thoughts toward responsibility.

More stories and resources available at karenholcombbooks.com and proverbialkids.com.

Don't Be Lazy or Rude Bible Stories

◆ Cain's Attitude— Genesis 4:1-15

Adam and Eve's sons, Cain grew up to be a gardener; Abel, a shepherd. In time, they each brought God an offering. Genesis 4:4 indicates that Abel's gift was sacrificial and sincere, given out of respect and love. But Cain's gift was out of obligation, with no sacrifice and little love. Self-centered, Cain became furious when he saw that God was pleased with Abel's gift but not his. God reasoned with him (v. 6-7), but Cain's anger escalated, and he murdered his brother. When God confronted him, Cain responded rudely, "Am I my brother's keeper?" Cain had a bad attitude that could have been lifted had he heeded God's counsel in 4:6-7. Share these verses with your children, encouraging them to "master sin" and avoid throwing pity parties!

◆ Nabal's Insults— 1 Samuel 25:2-42

Rich, successful, and *rude*—Nabal the Calebite was shearing sheep in Carmel when David and his soldiers set up camp in the nearby wilderness, on the run from King Saul. David sent a respectful greeting to the wealthy man, with a message that told how he and his men had protected the man's shepherds throughout their stay in Carmel. Then David asked Nabal if he could spare some food and provisions for his soldiers. 1 Samuel 25:9-11 contains Nabal's response. He insulted David and his men and treated them like dirt. Using the word "my" repeatedly, Nabal took credit for everything he owned, with no acknowledgment of God's blessing. A prime example of rudeness, this story continues to the end of chapter 25. Share it with your kids, contrasting Nabal's rudeness to his wife Abigail's prudent respectfulness.

◆ 3 Men's Talents— Matthew 25:14-30

This Parable of the Talents which Jesus taught urges believers to use all God has given them to grow His kingdom. It also applies to general work ethic. Matthew 25:14 begins with the Master dispersing talents/money before departing on a trip. The first two recipients took initiative and multiplied their Master's money, respective to their abilities. At his return, their Master was very pleased and rewarded them generously! The third man had buried his money in a hole in the ground and had nothing to show for the time that had passed. Rudely defensive, he stood before his Master and began accusing him of injustice. He made excuses. The Master had no good words for him. In God's kingdom, there is no place for laziness or rudeness!

◆ 10 Girls' Lamps—Matthew 25:1-13

Jesus' Parable of the Ten Virgins contrasts wise and foolish behavior and is ultimately a warning to be prepared for His Second Coming. Read this simple story in Matthew 25:1-13 to your family. Discuss the importance of being prepared for events & activities which are in the near future. Review v. 9, in which the unprepared girls ask to borrow oil, but the wise answered, "No." We should not expect to lean on others every time we are unprepared. Help your kids understand the concept of a deadline, goal-setting, & using time wisely. Explain eternal preparation through salvation, too!

Find these verses in your Bible and write them on a separate sheet.

Proverbs

6:6-8,10-11 (lazy)
15:12,19 (lazy)
19:15,24 (lazy)
21:24
22:10
22:13 (lazy)
24:30-34 (lazy)
26:16,18-19

See also 10 Commandment #3 & #4, and James 1:19-24; 2:14-17; and 3:13.

HOMEWork for Parents

Teach your kids to be diligent this week, learning to:

-take initiative when something needs to be done
-be observant of needs
-finish what is started
-look/plan ahead
-no be wasteful
-appreciate the production of goods

Practice manners to combat rudeness!

Welcome! Read the following plan carefully, along with the topical paragraph on page (vi). Prayerfully select one Opening Activity and one Bible Lesson to lead. Record Proverbs passages on a separate sheet. Begin with the Activity, share the Key Verse and the Bible story. Supplement with Wisdom in Babylon and Q & A. See the suggested reading list for additional resources on these ABC topics.

Enjoy God's Wisdom

Key Verse: *For the LORD gives wisdom; from his mouth come knowledge and understanding. He holds success in store for the upright, he is a shield to those whose walk is blameless …* Proverbs 2:6-8

Opening Activity— Perfect Plans Choose one activity.

Protected!— Make swords/shields out of cardboard & foil to illustrate the protective nature of God's wisdom.

Puzzled— Put together two 50-piece puzzles, swapping 5-6 pieces from each in advance, to illustrate life's unknowns.

All Your Heart— Print Proverbs 3:5-6 on a red heart. Cut into pieces; hide. Lead kids to find pieces and reconstruct heart.

A-Mazing Plans— Use masking tape/chalk to create a maze on a concrete surface. Walk through in pairs or individually.

Bible Lesson Choose one story.

Read the passage and highlights noted on the adjacent page; prepare to tell the story in your own words, emphasizing God's wisdom and knowledge. Share all Proverbs verses and Jeremiah 29:11. Use the Q & A below to supplement your teaching. On the fourth study, offer an invitation to all to accept Jesus as Savior.

- **God's Creation—** Genesis 1-2
- **The Tabernacle's Construction—** Exodus 25-30; 31:1-11
- **A Psalmist's Love—** Psalm 119:97-105; Exodus 20
- **God's Plan of Salvation—** 1 Cor. 1:30-31; John 3:16-17

Wisdom in Babylon

The prophet Daniel and his Israelite friends were facing death when Daniel prayed the prayer recorded in Daniel 2:20-23. King Nebuchadnezzar of Babylon had a confusing dream which he demanded his wise men to both recount and interpret. None of his Babylonian staff could do such an impossible thing. Only God could, and Daniel knew it. **Read aloud Dan. 2:20-23 and create a mural of these elements in Daniel's prayer: the Name of God, Time & Eternity, Wisdom, Power, Seasons, Kings & Thrones, Light & Darkness, and Thanksgiving.** Note: God answered this prayer! (See Daniel 2:31-45)

Q & A

⇒ What is this story about?
⇒ How did God show His wisdom in this story?
⇒ How has God given you wisdom before?
⇒ When the people followed God's leadership, were they successful? Explain.

Suggested Reading

Enjoy God's wisdom through the insight of others! The following helpful books were consulted for this project and may also be valuable to you in parenting:

Boundaries, by Drs. Henry Cloud & John Townsend (Zondervan)
30 Days to Taming Your Tongue, by Deborah S. Pegues (Harvest House)
Simple Life, by Thom & Art Rainer (Broadman & Holman)
Have a New Teenager by Friday, by Dr. Kevin Leman (Revell)
Love Dare for Parents, by Stephen & Alex Kendrick, *with Lawrence* Kimbrough (Broadman & Holman)

See karenholcombbooks.com and proverbialkids.com for new additions to the Proverbial Kids storybook collection.

Enjoy God's Wisdom Bible Stories

◆ God's Creation— Genesis 1-2

The Genesis 1 account of God's creation of the world is supported by passages in Job, Isaiah, Psalms, John, Romans, Colossians, Hebrews, Revelation, and referenced by Jesus in Mark 13:19. Creation's natural beauty and order are God's general revelation to humankind of His existence, His wisdom and goodness. He created time, space, energy, living and nonliving things, and natural and moral law. Many times God used the word *good* to describe His work. Share the Creation account with your children with confidence in this foundational truth. Marvel at the tiniest seed God placed inside a plant (1:11), at variations within species which produce like-kinded offspring (1:21, 24). Join the psalmist in praise to God whose glory is declared daily by the stars and planets (Ps. 19) held in place by His great power (Job 38:31).

◆ The Tabernacle's Construction— Exodus 25-30; 31:1-11

God shared His creative skill with those artisans who were commissioned to build a dwelling place for Him among His people, Israel. He called and gifted Bezaleel specifically for this purpose, filling him "with the Spirit of God, in wisdom, in understanding, in knowledge, and in all manner of workmanship" (See Ex. 31:1-5). In design, metal and jewel workmanship, carving and carpentry, Bezaleel led the construction of the Tabernacle and all of its utensils, furniture, sinks, coverings, and priestly garments. God also gifted Bezaleel's assistants. Chapters 25-30 contain God's instructions for this monumental task. Read the subheading from these chapters to become familiar with these items, describing them to your children. Acknowledge God as the source of wisdom for these creative abilities.

◆ A Psalmist's Love— Psalm 119; Exodus 20

In acrostic form, the unnamed writer of Psalm 119 used the letters of the Hebrew alphabet to begin each stanza of this psalm, in praise of God and His word. Introduce this psalm to your children and read aloud v. 97-105, an oft-quoted segment. This writer has obeyed God's commandments and experienced the joy of having a right relationship with God and others. Help your kids understand how he could *love a law*, describing God's word as sweet like honey. Turn to Exodus 20 in your Bible and read aloud the 10 Commandments. Discuss how they protect us and help us love God and others.

◆ God's Plan of Salvation— Genesis 3:15; John 3:16-17; 1 Corinthians 1:30-31; Hebrews 1:1-3

God warned Satan in the Garden of Eden that a "Seed" (child born) of a woman would one day crush his head because of his temptation of Adam and Eve. God foretold in Numbers 24:17 that a "Star" would come from Israel which would destroy wickedness. Prophets Micah, Daniel, Isaiah, Jeremiah, Hosea, and others prophesied details of the coming Savior's birth—all fulfilled in Jesus Christ, the "radiance" of God's glory (Hebrews 1:1-3). This is the Gospel message of John 3:16. Read aloud Genesis 3:15 and John 3:16 to your children. In His great wisdom, God chose to save a sinful world through the sinless life, death, burial, and resurrection of Jesus, "the power and wisdom of God" (1 Cor. 1:24). If we accept God's gift, we can be forgiven of our sins and spend eternity in heaven with God.

Find these verses in your Bible and write them on a separate sheet.

Proverbs

1:20-23	15:22
2:9-11	16:2-9,20
3:5-6	19:21
10:22,27-29	21:1
12:28	

See also the 10 Commandments and James 1:5 & 17.

HOMEWork for Parents

Work on your "vertical" relationship with God this week and your "horizontal" relationships with family members and others by:

-memorizing the 10 Commandments (Ex. 20)
-exercising the Fruit of the Spirit (Gal. 5:22-23)

Welcome! Read the following plan carefully, along with the topical paragraph on page (vi). Prayerfully select one Opening Activity and one Bible Lesson to lead. Record Proverbs passages on a separate sheet. Begin with the Activity, share the Key Verse and the Bible story. Supplement with the Game/Word Study and Q & A. Obtain the character storybook suggested below to read aloud with your children.

Forfeit Fortune & Fame for Faith, Family, & Friendship

Key Verses: *Better a dry crust with peace and quiet than a house full of feasting with strife.* Proverbs 17:1
Charm is deceptive and beauty is fleeting; but a woman who fears the LORD is to be praised. Proverbs 31:30

Opening Activity— Give it Over! Choose one activity.

Time Out!— Cancel your plans for a busy evening out, spread a blanket on the floor, and have a pizza crust picnic!

Marbles for Money— Coat marbles w/dishwashing liquid. Compete to grasp the most marbles for 5 seconds, overhanded.

Fleeting Beauty— Compare model photos in fashion & retirement magazines. Name older ladies who are praiseworthy.

Trust Fall— Illustrate trusting God by letting small individuals fall backward into the outstretched arms of adults.

Bible Lesson Choose one story.

Read the passage and highlights noted on the adjacent page; prepare to tell the story in your own words, providing additional context as needed. Use the Key Verses, Proverbs, and the Q & A below to supplement your teaching. (Note: *Forfeit* is used in this principle because an exchange takes place.)

- ♦ *A Mom's Legacy—* Proverbs 31
- ♦ *John's Stage—* Mark 1:1-8
- ♦ *A Lady's Perfume—* John 12:1-8; Mark 14:3-9
- ♦ *Paul's Contentment—* Acts 27, 2 Cor. 11

Passionate Pursuits...

- ♦ Enjoy a game of "Chase" with your family. Discuss the dangers of chasing wealth and fame.
- ♦ View a plant which has been overtaken by weeds or thorns. Discuss how busy-ness can stunt spiritual growth. (Matthew 13:22)

Content vs. Contentious

Write these two words on a dry erase board. Say, **These two words may look alike, but they are opposites! To be content means to be satisfied; where as to be contentious (root word contend) means to argue a lot—something James 4:1-3 links to having wrongful desires.**

(See other related verses in Proverbs.)

Q & A

⇒ Who is this story about?
⇒ In what way did that person trust God? What was the end result of his/her trust?
⇒ Which did he/she forfeit for God: Fortune, Fame, or Both?

Character Book

Contentious Adeline and the Rooftop Escape is about a little girl who idolizes her monthly *Pretty Palace* magazine. When Grandpa builds a treehouse, Adeline expects her brothers to paint & decorate it accordingly. Their pushback brings Adeline to tears until her father steps in, giving her the listening ear she's been longing for. Verses from Proverbs offer wisdom over materialism and discord.

More stories and resources available at
karenholcombbooks.com **and** proverbialkids.com.

Forfeit Fortune & Fame Bible Stories

◆ A Mom's Legacy— Proverbs 31

Written by King Lemuel (possibly another name for Solomon), Proverbs 31 describes a virtuous wife and mother. She is respectful, industrious, conscientious, strong, intelligent, and merciful. Verses 10-31 paint the picture of a woman thriving in her relationships and completely committed to her family, home, and community. Her children and her husband love her! The writer concludes in verses 30-31 that the virtuous woman's fear of the LORD is more praiseworthy than deceitful charm and superficial beauty, and she should be rewarded with gifts and praise! As you share this chapter with your daughters, encourage them to develop these virtues; with your sons, encourage them to appreciate them!

◆ John's Stage— Mark 1:1-8

Perhaps the most pivotal character in the Bible apart from Christ was John the Baptist. Prophesied about hundreds of years before his birth (Isaiah 40:3), John stepped onto Earth's stage without a stage—no city stage, no glitzy ad campaign, no big paycheck or fan club. Crying out his message in the Judean wilderness, dressed in camel hair, eating locusts and wild honey, John lived free from fleshly entrapments and accomplished God's will for his life. Share his story with your family, encouraging your older children to forfeit fortune and fame for God's will in their lives. Help them be content with His provision and anticipate His good plan for their lives. Enjoy real relationships!

◆ A Lady's Perfume— John 12:1-8

Broken and spilled out. Days before the Passover, Jesus went to the home of his friends Lazarus, Martha, and Mary to dine with them before going on to Jerusalem, where He would be arrested and crucified. While Martha served and Lazarus reclined with Jesus at the table, Mary brought an alabaster jar of very expensive perfume into the room, broke it open, and wiped His feet with her hair. Her act of worship not only prepared Jesus' body for burial, it also communicated her own surrender. Mary gave the beautiful fragrance to Jesus, rather than saving it for herself. In Old Testament times, when a sink was needed for the Tabernacle, some women donated their bronze mirrors—no small gift (Ex. 38:8). God is worthy of all praise! Giving treasures to Him out of love exalts Him to the proper place in our hearts!

◆ Paul's Contentment— Acts 27; 2 Corinthians 11; Philippians 3; Ecclesiastes 2

Exchanging personal glory (Phil. 3:5-7) for a life of servanthood, the Apostle Paul survived danger and extreme need for the family of God (2 Cor. 11), yet he testified in his letter to the church at Philippi that he was content in all things! Near the end of his ministry, Paul was arrested in Jerusalem and sent by ship to Italy, where he was to stand trial before Rome's Caesar. Read Acts 27 and tell the shipwreck story in your own words as one example of Paul's perils. Forfeiting his own glory and comfort, Paul found contentment and joy (Phil. 4:10-11). Although King Solomon lived his latter years for his own pleasure, with regret, the king also concluded that joy comes from God (Eccl. 2:26)—not fortune and fame!

Find these verses in your Bible & write them on a separate sheet.

Proverbs

10:7	15:16-17
11:28-29	17:17,24-25
12:11	23:4-5
13:12	25:24
14:1,30	27:8-9,23-24

See also 10 Commandment #2, #4, #5, & #10 and James 1:2-4; 3:16-18.

HOMEWork for Parents

Set an example of contentment this week!

-Slow down
-Seek the Lord, inviting Him to guide your parenting
-Search your heart, surrendering your pursuits & goals to God
-Make your home sweet and welcoming in a tangible way
-Keep your promises to your children!

TEACHING PLAN – G

Welcome! Read the following plan carefully, along with the topical paragraph on page (vi). Prayerfully select one Opening Activity and one Bible Lesson to lead. Record Proverbs passages on a separate sheet. Begin with the Activity, share the Key Verse and the Bible story. Supplement with the Object Lesson and Q & A. Obtain the character storybook suggested below to read aloud with your children.

Gain Honestly

Key Verses: *The LORD detests dishonest scales, but accurate weights find favor with him.* Proverbs 11:1
Dishonest money dwindles away, but whoever gathers money little by little makes it grow. Proverbs 13:11

Opening Activity— Honestly? Choose one activity.

Sneaky Thief!— Lead group to play money-making board game. Secretly designate a "thief" who should seek to win.

Scale Mischief— Announce you will be weighing everyone. In advance/throughout, skew scale mechanism by 8-15 lbs.

Good Gain— Tour a local business or observe an occupation online. Help children recognize work that warrants pay.

Work Project— Do a non-paid act of kindness for a needy individual/family. Discuss the rewarding nature of volunteering.

Bible Lesson Choose one story.

Read the passage & highlights noted on the adjacent page; prepare to tell the story in your own words. (The object lesson below will help children understand the concept of using unjust weights as a means of theft.) Use the Scripture verses and the Q & A below to supplement your teaching.

- ◆ **Jeremiah's Payment—** Jeremiah 32
- ◆ **A Family's Deceit—** Genesis 27:1-40
- ◆ **God's House—** Mark 11:15-17
- ◆ **Zacchaeus' Decision—** Luke 19:1-10

Object Lesson

In advance, obtain two identical half-gallon pitchers with lids and two dozen doughnuts. Put an airtight bag of rocks in one of the pitchers, then fill both with water, until they are of equal weight. Provide each team with several 3-oz cups.

To begin your object lesson, divide your family/group in two, and give each a pitcher. Explain that you are very thirsty and are exchanging one doughnut for 2 cups of water. Begin the exchange! When it becomes noticeable that one team has been cheated, reveal the deception! Explain that "weighted" scales were used in Bible times for dishonest exchanges.

Q & A

⇒ Who is this story about? Was this an honest person?
⇒ Through what actions did this person make his/her money?
⇒ What are some things other than money that people are eager to gain?

Character Books

Look for **Honest Oliver's Terribly Tempting Opportunity** under Proverbial Kids Short Stories at www.proverbialkids.com.

Gain Honestly Bible Stories

◆ Jeremiah's Payment— Jeremiah 32

Identical pans suspended on opposite ends of a bar and balanced on a fulcrum, *scales of justice* ensure an exact measure. Items in one pan are counter-balanced with standard weights in the other. In Deuteronomy 25:13-15, God commanded perfect and just weights to be used in trade. In Jeremiah 32, He told the prophet Jeremiah to purchase a field from his cousin. Jeremiah weighed the payment carefully in front of witnesses and paid full price—all this, knowing the land was under siege by the Babylonians. The prophet could have been tempted to be dishonest, fearing the purchase to be a loss. But he was honest and trusted God with Israel's future. Share this story with your children. Instill an understanding of God's sovereign nature. Teach them to gain honestly in trading with their friends & siblings. If led by the Holy Spirit, describe God's just act in giving His own sinless Son as the balancing sacrifice for sinful humanity.

◆ A Family's Deceit— Genesis 27:1-40

Twins, Esau and Jacob were the sons of Isaac and Rebekah. Grasping his brother's heel at birth, Jacob appeared jealous of his firstborn twin even as a baby. Genesis 25:27-28 plainly tells that the parents played favorites with these two boys. Isaac favored Esau; Rebekah, Jacob. As a young man, Jacob stole Esau's birthright through an unfair trade. Years later, Rebekah devised a plan to deceive her dying husband into giving his parting blessing to Jacob, rather than Esau. Summarize Genesis 27 for your children. Jacob followed through with the lie. He dishonestly gained his father's blessing, causing much family grief. Jacob himself was later deceived by his father-in-law and by his own jealous sons. Favoritism crushes children! Dishonest gain is loss! The good news? Reconciliation is possible! See Genesis 33.

◆ God's House— Mark 11:15-17

The Temple in Jerusalem was built for the worship of God, not for personal gain. In Mark 11:15-17, greedy business men and bankers had set up booths in the Temple, selling items like doves, grain, and oil to poor Jews who would then offer them as sacrifices to God for their sins. When Jesus arrived in Jerusalem days before His crucifixion, He entered the Temple and confronted these men. Read aloud v. 15-17. From Jesus' words, we glean that they were overcharging their customers and cheating them with falsified scales. Though selling products is often restricted in our modern church, we still must teach our children to resist using the worship setting as an opportunity for personal gain—money or attention—coming before the Lord with a pure heart.

◆ Zacchaeus' Decision— Luke 19:1-10

A chief tax-collector, Zacchaeus had a bad reputation for cheating, charging people much more than they really owed and keeping a large cut for himself. When he heard Jesus was in Jericho, Zacchaeus climbed a tree along the crowded street to see Him. When Jesus spoke to him and told him He would be eating supper with him, Zacchaeus welcomed Him gladly. In a short period of time, Zacchaeus knew he needed to make things right with the people he had cheated. He surrendered his worldly wealth for a relationship with God, paying back four times what he owed. Jesus celebrated that salvation came to Zacchaeus that day. After sharing this story with your children, invite them to confess their own dishonest actions, seek God's forgiveness, and (if they haven't done so already) invite Jesus to be their Lord and Savior.

Find these verses in your Bible & write them on a separate sheet.

Proverbs

6:12-15	15:27
11:16, 24-25	17:23
12:11, 14	20:10
13:11	21:6

See also 10 Commandment #6 & #9 and James 5:1-5

HOMEWork for Parents

Talk with your children about the importance of being honest in:

-counting & measuring	-remembering
-trading	-answering questions &
-playing Games	-earning rewards.
-testing	

Help them understand that dishonesty does not bring peace, but guilt and trouble.

Proverbial Kids Character Books

Little Jimmy and the Spoiled Rotten Banana
Captain Curious and the Invisible Boundary Line
Look-at-Me Lucy and the Rearview Mirror
Contentious Adeline and the Rooftop Escape
Lazy Leo's Totally Untapped Talent
Available at www.westbowpress.com and Amazon.
Look for these Proverbial Kids short stories coming soon to www.proverbialkids.com.
Verbose Verbena's Backfire Advice
Dexter's Do-it-Yourself Disaster
The Tri-County RUDEsters' Most Amazing Home Run!
Honest Oliver's Terribly Tempting Opportunity (wt)

Small-Group 8-week Study Format

Session 1

Preparation: Obtain copies of this resource for all participants and encourage them to bring it to each small- group session. Copy & cut apart the **7 ABCs Bookmarks** on the adjacent page.

Welcome & Ice Breaker—In pairs, create an ABC acrostic of concerns you have in parenting, for which you need wisdom.

Bible Verse—Share Proverbs 3:5-6 and James 1:5.

Prayer for Wisdom in Parenting

Introduction—Refer to page (iv) to introduce this resource. Give each participant a copy of the **Bookmark** or list the 7 ABCs on a dry erase board. Read aloud the **A-Accept Instruction** intro on page (v) and review the other ABCs, noting the principles are applicable for all ages.

Bible Time—Call on volunteers with Bibles to find and read aloud the Proverbs verses referenced at the bottom of the righthand page in the plan. Discuss each. Share the "God's Parenting" Bible Story and highlights from the other three stories.

Group Time—Divide into small groups to review the **A** lesson plan and determine possible ways to use it at home this week. Share with large group.

Character Books—Display the character books available for reinforcing the theme with their children. Read one aloud if desired!

Challenge—Challenge each family to use the **A** plan at home this week and do the HOMEWork for Parents. Suggest participants hold each other accountable.

Conclude—Close in prayer for each parent to follow God's lead in wise parenting.

Sessions 2-8

Preparation: Preview all Proverbs verses for the upcoming session, asking God for insight in teaching. See www.proverbialkids.com for additional resources.

Welcome/Cheers & Challenges—Welcome all! Invite participants to share successful, champion-building/challenging teaching moments from the past week of parenting, along with how they used the lesson plan.

Ice Breaker—Select one of the Opening Activities from this session's lesson plan and lead it with your small group.

Prayer—Praise God for His great wisdom and ask that He grant wisdom to your small group participants.

Refer to the **B** (C, D, E, F, or G) plan. Share the introductory paragraph on page (v-vi). Read aloud the **Key Verse** from the plan and call for volunteers to read aloud the Proverbs verses referenced at the bottom of the righthand page in the plan. Discuss each. Share the opening Bible Story at the top of the page and highlights from the other three stories.

Share your own experience related to this topic and read aloud the theme's **Character Book.**

HOMEWork for Parents—Read aloud the short assignment. Challenge participants to continue training champions this week using the **B** (C, D, E, F, or G) plan.

Conclude— Close session with Prayer. Consider having a group social event following the final session.

See www.proverbialkids.com
for additional resources.

7 ABCs
for Parenting

Proverbial Kids©
Wisdom for Young Families

 A — **Accept Instruction**
Proverbs 1:8-9

 B — **Be Humble & Kind**
Proverbs 27:2, 19:17

 C — **Control Your Curiosity & Your Tongue**
Proverbs 5:15, 10:19b

 D — **Don't be Lazy or Rude**
Proverbs 10:4, 29:21

 E — **Enjoy God's Wisdom**
Proverbs 2:6-8

 F — **Forfeit Fortune & Fame**
for Faith, Family, & Friendship
Proverbs 17:1, 31:30

 G — **Gain Honestly**
Proverbs 11:1, 13:11

Karenholcombbooks.com
www.proverbialkids.com

7 ABCs
for Parenting

Proverbial Kids©
Wisdom for Young Families

A — **Accept Instruction**
Proverbs 1:8-9

B — **Be Humble & Kind**
Proverbs 27:2, 19:17

C — **Control Your Curiosity & Your Tongue**
Proverbs 5:15, 10:19b

D — **Don't be Lazy or Rude**
Proverbs 10:4, 29:21

E — **Enjoy God's Wisdom**
Proverbs 2:6-8

F — **Forfeit Fortune & Fame**
for Faith, Family, & Friendship
Proverbs 17:1, 31:30

G — **Gain Honestly**
Proverbs 11:1, 13:11

Karenholcombbooks.com
www.proverbialkids.com

7 ABCs
for Parenting

Proverbial Kids©
Wisdom for Young Families

  A — **Accept Instruction**
Proverbs 1:8-9

B — **Be Humble & Kind**
Proverbs 27:2, 19:17

 C — **Control Your Curiosity & Your Tongue**
Proverbs 5:15, 10:19b

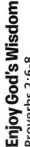 **D** — **Don't be Lazy or Rude**
Proverbs 10:4, 29:21

 **E** — **Enjoy God's Wisdom**
Proverbs 2:6-8

F — **Forfeit Fortune & Fame**
for Faith, Family, & Friendship
Proverbs 17:1, 31:30

 G — **Gain Honestly**
Proverbs 11:1, 13:11

Karenholcombbooks.com
www.proverbialkids.com

Printed in the United States
By Bookmasters